SAY THE WORD

AJ SAUR

murmuration
press™

Book design: Amy Cole
Cover photo: Phalakon Jaisangat

ISBN: 978-1-946671-12-7

Printed in the United States of America

Body text is typeset in Adobe Garamond. Headings are typeset in ABeeZee

Murmuration Press

To contact the publisher concerning this book or others like it, email:
murmurationpress@gmail.com

For The Ready
and SDG

TABLE OF CONTENTS

DOWNWARD

UPWARD

— INWARD —

Acknowledgements

DOWNWARD

ANIMATE
\\'a-nə-ˌmāt\\

You birthed in words
said aloud: *visage,*
paradigm, epitome—

my breath the seed,
you the soil, the spring
rain, the sprout.

What about the complete sentence?
The spaces
not incorporeal but full

of intercostal muscles, memories
allowing, at last,
the exhale.

Where's my place
in this chest-rise,
fall?

Entire paragraphs
supposedly alive within
my diaphragm and fertile.

Where then the growing
vine tendrilling
my head and heart

if your form realized
reforms the human line? Am I
an embedded clause, dead,

as dropped leaves,
or spine-broken as a rake
unable to heap heat?

What of *fecundity*,
of *resuscitation*—
those future tenses

at ease
in the lift of branches.
How short

my tome
when cold seizes—a blank-
faced stare reaching nowhere.

BAPTISM

\\'bap-,ti-zəm\\

She didn't know it then
that he'd never be closer
than those first nine months.
Only later did she wonder

if that's why she carried him so high,
right below her heart, his toes
barely skimming her waistline.
If he had reached up

with his forming fingers,
he could have climbed her rib cage
like a jungle gym
and nestled in her throat—a lump

the same size as the one
she's currently trying to swallow.
For today he becomes
someone else's son—

held secure, just briefly,
in the wet womb of another
skimming his toes
on a rocky riverbed.

He'll reach up
his calloused hands,
scale her darkness,
emerge her radiant child.

She wills herself to be happy
but as he slips under
out of reach, she clutches
her hands to her breast

feeling there
an indention
and a lone beating
heart.

COURSE
\\'kȯrs\\

Coming to this riverside,
could it be me who runs swiftly
while the water stands banked
at my attention?

Might it be like coming to
from a dream in which I am bent
and bent until bowed? But not at
some predictable end.

Jesus said, *See to the hungry,*
the outcast, the washed up ones.
Dear Lord, there's so much flooding
I'm unfastened and torrenting.

What's steadfast
if the place you're headed
we can't come? Why give a damn
if every table spread

floats away
until we're all aimlessly eating
our own bread and fishes?
Funny how your last supper fixed nothing

to shore, only made us aware
of our dining alone.
Not unlike, I suspect, the way you felt
in that first and later garden

where every river was hidden
in trees unsoundly asleep.
I awoke this morning
to my own weeping, tears streaming

as if a spring of life
was trying to remind me
that everything in motion
is moved.

DROUGHT
\'draut\

The dark hued house stews
under a sanguine sun,
the potted plants
on the front porch
shrink back.

Having no defense
from so much cheer,
the grass in the yard has died
to cloud-filled dreams, the hope
of a tracing shadow.

I go to my room, pull the curtains,
lay low, press ear
against pressed wood
listening for coolness,
for the possibility of relief.

I want to believe in rain,
in hard drops that won't kill you.
But pain promises nothing, cares not
for the prayers of those with a face
planted in floorboards.

What grows there is supple, though,
opening each day
to a sky so full of itself,
to an expectancy in the unknowing—
surviving the too muchness,

thriving in the going
without.

EPOCH
  \'e-,päk\

  A cloud received Him out of sight. ~ Acts 1:9

The space between
tomorrow and today,
which is to say, the distance
from you to me,

spans mere millimeters—
the interval between the C3
and C4 vertebrae
when the head lifts

to cloudy sky
more in wonder of a rising
than certain
of what happens next.

Not an appearing,
at least as of yet,
just a clearing—
the lengthening of neck

to spy new places,
a gap
extending
beyond earth's end.

The standing, the gaping
seems so easy now
when faced
with an age outstretched—

an unending promise
unfulfilled.
Still, the heart
hears the words

of the two beings in white
who know what it means
to descend.
Yet, they have no idea

of the area we must cover—
the aperture
of our bodies,
the way my bending

may not move me
far enough
like the heads
of the rhododendron

hanging low
after heavy rains
almost kissing the ground,
but not quite.

FOUNTAINHEAD
\\'faủn-tᵊn-,hed\\

If we trace
this river to its source,
what will we discover?
A bubbling up

from some unseen
place or perhaps
the eternal embrace
of eager lovers—

an entwined heartbeat
pumping the flow,
sowing
a thousand tributaries.

What's begun, though,
isn't contained knowing
as if we can bank
the feel of water on skin

spend it
whenever a distance
grows between us.
The intentional

immersion releases us
from the fixed notion
of feet, of a landedness
in which we control

every bend of flesh,
every poised muscle.
After all,
doesn't the sweetest fruit

lend itself to limb,
swim with the current,
stem any stream
of independence?

In due course,
it will find its end
in the mouth of one
who will savor its richness,

let the wine run freely
down chin, onto collar
until everything's soaked clean
through with it.

GARDEN
\\ˈgär-dᵊn\\

How easily the skin gives way
to teeth, bonds of atoms loosened,
then tightened in a lone bite. Only after
can they see the naked flesh—

how supple it is, how it bends
and curves to both reveal
and conceal. That's the curse
of eyes, to steal a glance

like King David on the rooftop
after he wilted on war.
Jesus' disciples also knew
the heaviness of sight

when asked to keep watch, pour
themselves out in prayer.
Who could blame them
for falling asleep

surrounded by trees that bore no fruit.
No scent of olive or pear,
no plum to press against lips
in the dead of night.

Only Christ stayed awake
to accept the cup of wrath and shame—
a ferment of crushed grapes
sweating red.

It seems even the vine
has something to prove—
entangled in this mess
of temptation.

The rose's role is yet
to be seen, though the soul
can already follow the plot line—
that hedge we edge toward

pulling at petals, climbing
down stems, turning
over leaves until settled
in the cool dirt.

HAND

\\'hand\\

Not even a whole one appeared
to write some words on a wall—
just a few fingers were enough
to set the king's knees knocking.
Forget trying to lock the door

as if we could stop the reaching through
and into. Few are as blessed
as Jacob whose cleaving
caught hold of God anew.
Even Jesus' went slack

when kissed goodnight in the garden.
I guess a fist, a sword-swinging wrist
don't figure into this plan.
We all must travel a dark
expanse, those three hours unraveling

eternity until we're back
climbing a tree, picking
fruit, waving gratitude
to the passerby who sowed
the sun, harvested the sky,

raised his in return.

INCARNATION
\,in-(,)kär-ˈnā-shən\

Every wave has two ends
and both may be invisible
to the human eye.

This could explain why
I never saw your cresting,
never received

your sent messages.
Hovering over water's surface
is one thing, being moved,

another. No longer other
the short frequency of days
leaves me frantic to find you

in the visible range.
How strange, then
to discover   her

bent over a toilet bowl,
darkness churning into light.
What a wonder

her turning spectrum
to sight—the right angle
of you

prisming
even the night into
a billion spectacular stars.

I am here now
holding her hand
tying us together

as the sea rolls and has its say—
three days in the belly,
three days hugging the shore,

a seventh to rest, to reflect
each morning each evening
and then set out again searching

for one curve more.

JESUS

\ˈjē-zəs\

In beginning a poem about the only begotten God
let your letting be as loose as hands bound in prayer
grasping the pen as if beholden to more
than mere truth like the catch in the chest
when your beloved appears at last
at the far horizon of the terminal and you run
on without the impediment of punctuation
or that unction of discourse interested in your own
elegance of stride and not the end
when what you long for is that first kiss
of the Word on your lips
his hand on your neck a novel you forever reread
not heeding the coffee on his breath
instead fixed on that tongue that quenches
as though a new language in your mouth moves
your entire body with such a fluttering of flesh
you wonder if the dove descended or you arose
on some bright wing of syllables not your own
the way a kite mesmerizes with its dips and rises
how that tail dances its inexplicable dance—and never lets go

KEEPER
\'kē-pər\

Judas kept his head
as he led a band of soldiers
through the garden darkness.

No foot slipped as if a kiss
had fixed their field of vision
floating them over uncovered root,

the trip of a fallen apple. Still,
he clutched his purse in trust
of the coin's smooth edge

finding relief in Caesar.
So lovely that dwelling place
he sought, some piece of land to look out on—

a lasting impression of one possessed
by his duty. With unblinking eyes
he set his face toward its end

and even when history dashes him
against the rocks, he stays the course
through those midnight trees

intent on reaching Jesus first.
And he does
lean in as one dearly beloved,

but glances off
that treasured chest,
his head forever arrested

in a noose, his feet
always inches above

hallowed ground.

LIBATION
\lī-'bā-shən\

How light these glasses we raise
to ring in the New Year
or praise the newlyweds whose lips
hold love with such ease—
an effervescent tease of gravity
with the lift of a wrist.

But that's levitation—a turn
of ulna and radius to elevate a kiss
of sky as if the stars are saturated
with a brightness we can wring,
swallow to not die like this.
How satisfying to progress

beyond down,
the enlightened now floating
on fancy cruise ships—
sliding it all in to win big
at roulette or pooling chips
to bet on their highest hand.

The poor know their only play
is to cup their palms, catching
the next crush of grapes
from their own down-
trodden souls, then pour out
on the dry dirt. First in—

legs, then torso, sinking arm,
unbent elbow, finally, bowed
head until quenched,
save the red wine stain
on the turned-down collar
of the groom's festal shirt.

MONOLITH
\'mä-nə-ˌlith\

Man alone carves in stone
a lineage of fame, a name,
a score of dates
marking everyone's end.

This goes as far back
as rocks go—us
chiseling out a life, scratching
at an itch we can't quite reach.

Everything's dust

the preacher jaws
grinding people finer than chaff
that the wind won't carry
to mountain top.

Everything's a laugh

we want to say
us dancing on our ancestors,
climbing to find something
that doesn't always rotate

and float away.
Even words on tablets cut
from sacred stone sans hands
can't stand the churn of time.

All will be thrown down

exclaims the Teacher
who descends
from his lofty pulpit
to look us square in the eyes.

Yet, we scale a lie—
that brimstone that seems
so high we bow
our whole weight into it.

How will we learn
to praise a pebble,
a barely perceptible pip
buried in soft tissue?

Those who fall on this stone
will be broken to pieces

claims the One
who smashes bits
into smaller bits
and then gathers all

on the tip
of some stylus, rests it
in a groove, lets loose a tune
that carries forever into space

building speed
like a child racing through a song
so she can sing it over again,

and again.

NAMING

\\'nām-iŋ\\

In a mother's cradle, a first glen,
the newborn's mouth opens
in an echo from that invisible land we know

as though we'd been there only yesterday.
And perhaps we were
at that moment before God came calling

when he brought each beast
and living thing for branding—
alligator, platypus, porcupine,

Adam flexing his pristine tongue
in a tumble of words
as if even the divine could get carried away.

And maybe he does get caught up
in trees, blushing like a Japanese maple,
swaying like a mountain hemlock.

He can't help opening the door
to the knock of the pileated woodpecker
and its abundance of syllables.

With creation so full
of flowing diphthongs, rolling Rs,
those pleasurable sibilants,

where can man find a side-
door to slip out
to locate a silent hollow—

a space to look up
at the nameless stars or down
at the bone-dry riverbed

where he can fall asleep
nestled in fresh silt,
dream of new flesh familiar

as a lover's whisper.

OUT
   \'aủt\

of darkness   an outline
traced on the bedroom floor
by a naked bulb overhead
heavy with light, drawing me in-
to its promise that every curve

will be love-handled
until one, beginning-to-end.

In such a place, am I free
to bend forward without
losing a feel for the familiar
footboard, the known creaks
of this mapped mattress?

Does the outward
require a casting off

of these gentle sheets, this body-
heated bed to discover that out-
lying world said to be true?
Here I go
though, wait, what's this

new cavity in me
yawning

for a form in daylight?
My moon-shape is
misaligned with sunshine,
this pour of blaze
creating me in its image.

It's a set-up.
I've been framed

like a door people can now enter
and exit at will. Where's my
down-feather pillow,
that soft ground
to cover ears, drown out

this constant flow
of opinions?

PROFANE
\prō-'fãn\

To say shit is to say nothing,
which is exactly what grandpa did
when staking tomato plants
in the garden plot behind his house.
Not that he didn't lay a bit of cow manure
on his potatoes every year. I would know
because I lugged a bag of it from the feed store

to the parking lot
where he sat silently staring out
of his Chevy truck. If he heard me curse
under my breath when heaving the bag
into the bed, he didn't note, though,
he never failed to slide a five spot
into my hand at the end of the day.

To speak shit is to lie,
which grandpa never did
even when grandma didn't exactly
catch him with his hand in the cookie jar.
How far the apple falls—me feigning
ignorance when grandma inquired after
my chocolate-covered lips.

To see is to know,
my grandparents' preacher used to say,
which was true for grandma. For grandpa,
to know was sight like those potatoes growing
quietly in the dark, like the fecundity
of a man consecrating a boy
with a feast from holy ground.

QUIVER
    \'kwi-vər\

The seven brothers threaded her

like a needle in order
to stitch a line that would last.

But it lacked
the necessary backing to be
pulled through, knotted forever.

They sought to hoop an heir from thin
material, but the binding severed
once, twice, seven times
until perfectly dead.

Finally, she also lost the point
of hanging by a string waiting
for God or fate to quilt a something
from nothing. She didn't unravel
in hate, just ceased singing lullabies

as she worked the edges—looping
over and over and over and over
and over and over and over
in sequenced rhythm. Even so
she embroidered to the end, sewing
those borders with flawless balance

of security and fall, never slipping
into false hope, never running
after rainbows. Perhaps she swaddled
after all—those abundant offspring
who continue
to admire her bearing air
their lips trembling to

hear

her

hum.

RIFT
     \'rift\

I am no goat, ram, or heifer—meat
placed on left or right, cut
in two for you to walk through.

You're smoke in the eyes
hiding my lying next to
never severed,
never a part of that Red Sea
you could plunge into.

If cleansed from leprosy,
the Law demands
a priest to see the skin
then slay a bird
over an earthen vessel

collect the blood
dip hyssop then
sprinkle.

Can it be that simple?
Slit the neck
to turn blue sky scarlet—
tying a thread from me to you
like an eternal covenant, like a thought

I thought I understood, like a string
holding tight to a slammed door's doorknob.
Toothless and without flight,
am I the unbroken broken—
a mourning dove awaiting

those flaming torches in the garden at night
or maybe, maybe the morning light
rending the horizon?

SACRIFICE
\\'sa-krə-,fis\\

Twine cut skin
as the wood was put
on his back, strapped tightly
with the kindling coarse
against neck's nape
when his head tilted up.

His father carried the knife
in his belt, cupped
the fire from wind
as they ascended.
Both knew heaviness
in the climb, felt life

drain from their limbs.
What did they hear
in the growing dark
when the foot slipped?
Sliding pebbles, the crash
of a nation, an almost

imperceptible voice
saying *Here I am?*
Who can help
but stash hope
in what's ahead—a rising
sun, a ram-snagging thicket,

a future outstretched and grasped
at the wrist?
Yet first
we must stack timber,
bind our beloveds,
prepare to burn.

THUMMIM

\\'thə-məm\\

The Babylonians stole our confidence.
Snatched it while we gazed back
at that laid waste temple. Some beast
of a man now bears the breastplate—

hangs it around his neck
like a victory wreath. Let's forget
the jewels, if we can. Let's pretend
gold tarnishes in that foreign land.

Who understands God's will?
Can choice be waylaid until it gives up
the truth, or is "yes" our only demand?
But an empty-handed promise

returns nothing. We can't ransom
with darkness—that space
between sacred ground and the toss
after it's carried off to Babylon.

Perhaps we'll discover found and lost
are two sides of the same stone we flip
again and again and again and again
as if we're bound together in this forever.

URIM

\,yу̇r-ə-m\

Cast your stone.
Toss it like you know
what you're doing.
A "no" is not knowing.
It's a two letter word.

Full stop.

We grow in concentric rings
like your slung rock in a lake—
each ripple a pondering.
But you want this rune to ruin you
so God's to blame.

Full stop.

A lot
becomes everything
if you look back—
a pillar of salt
filling a jar

fully. Stop

taking pleasure
in pickled peaches
as if consuming
the pits
can substitute for

fullness. Stop

falling into yourself
like an unwishing well.
Moses didn't fling coins.
He set gems in a breastplate
which covered the ephod

fully stopping

not the priestly heart
but willing it to wait until walls
are torn down, bricks thrown aside
and everyone outside is inside
passing the peace with a kiss

full, unstoppable

VANE
\'vān\

This cock doesn't crow three times,
just spins endlessly
chasing its tail feathers
targeting the flow of wind.

But its fletching lies
not flat, never flying off the bow
to achieve a perfect rotation. Still,
this betrayal hits its mark

or Peter, as in a similar case
which appears closed with a look—
one straight shaft shot
and the show's over.

Is that the point of sin
to pin us to the board
like a blue-tipped butterfly?
Bull's-eye

the archer cries
as if the arrow had an end,
as if the score
is already settled.

Bullshit
we want to utter
when the head turns
True North.

This is no knock on Jesus
whose faithful limbs pulled
taut the scarlet strings,
but on the hand that grips the gale

releases it with such abandon
we can't catch our breath
aren't east or west,
right or left

just wheel like a windmill
grinding the grain,
never humble enough
to stop

and savor.

WITNESS

\\'wit-nəs\\

There's a notch in Jesus' side
where you can get caught
as Thomas did, mouth snagged open

in disbelief, or belief.
Allure takes many shapes
usually shiny and sharp

as a diamond tip, or your eyes
in morning light.
Sight doesn't quite see

the V-shaped hollow you left
when you stole your body away.
This is love, my friends say,

this new groove in the heart
playing the same notes over and over and over
until the world gives in—

civilization spinning into
a single point of view, the only side
supposedly worth listening to.

What's more true—you or me?
Who gets the last word
if there's only one song?

I know you'll shake your head
when hearing this
and remark that I missed

what's directly in front of me.
Maybe so.
Or

perhaps the gap is a lie
and you're inside me
still.

EXIT
    \\'ek-sət\\

The Showbread sits precariously
on a gilded table that stretches its legs
like it's going to make a break
for the Holy of Holies.

Four legs hurry back from Emmaus
to offer the crumbs of a presence
now absent
they can't account for.

I can't explain the resurrected flesh,
its revelation of parts moving
this way and that. Supposedly
the heart swells when fresh,

but I fell flat trying to follow
the leavened path. Now I'm out on limbs
collecting manna—this morning's wafers
disappearing like dreams

the moment I consume them.
All I recall are the leaves, me dropping
everything to grasp at dimming ankles.
Was your body ever there?

Does anyone anywhere
comprehend this mystery
of rent crust, the rush of steam
                            rising?

YAW

\\'yȯ\\

You see, I saw

                a man

who was neither

                landed

nor lost at sea

                but rolling up

his sleeves

                to get down

to business.

                Of (a) course,

the fish felt set up,

                him casting his net

this way

                and that

yet always assured

                of a catch-

ed tailwind

                to his intended

destination.

                Is anything ever erratic

when you know

        the chart,

can turn

        every errant heart's

curve

        to the perfect tack?

It's easy for him

        to stand on the sea—legs

formed from the deep.

        I'm tossed

port

        to starboard

until there's no bearing

        just a sickness

you call love. Funny

        how the waves greet him,

but wave me off

        as if the sooner I die

the faster I find my way.

        It's that word *die*

that's dive-bombing

        my mind these days

because he also reeled

          in your storyline—

walked the planked path

          into the abyss.

Perhaps we're all caught

          in this mad

weaving

          such that

left

          right

mean less

          than this:

    Follow me.

ZENITH

\\'zē-nəth\\

I pretend not to see
the full spectrum.
As if the ending's
still a mystery, or
the beginning—
the way you found me

hidden below the horizon
of a Harry Potter book
at the downtown Starbucks.
I wonder now
did I raise my eyes
or were they drawn upward

by a spell—some incantation
of perfectly aligned words
bound between us?
But the source lacks clarity,
unlike poetry where one line
leads to the next,

or the neck,
if I remember correctly
the order of events,
me on your couch
then a phrase caught
in your throat.

Further in, I note the footboard,
the manner of your feet against it
as if ready for takeoff.
I guess I shouldn't be surprised
by your launch—the predictable
progression of waves, how they always

float away. I suppose
some also sip cappuccino
at trendy new cafés uptown—
ones with rainbow flags
in the window, hung
vertically.

UPWARD

ZOOM

\'züm\

I need a DeLorean,
a quaint main street, a stroke
of brilliance at 10:04 to find me
in the right spacetime. Continuums

are straight lines to follow
like a guitar strung taut
and strummed after kissing
one's mother for the last

first time. Fine is relative
until I'm fading
in that old Polaroid shot.
What I wouldn't give for thick wrists

and a perfectly-fitted headband
to rock through the night—
every clique and circle
basking in my burning licks.

But the circumference turns
until there's no way out,
even if reaching the ideal speed
the wheels won't reverse

to a present sans that new past
just lived.
When the clock clicks 10:03,
perhaps I need only this:

you grasping me
at the edge, lightly
shaking until
I fill the frame.

WHY

\ '(h)wī \

Someone once said that art exists in the asking
of questions that go unanswered in the end.
As if I could explain the honey bee

and her generosity to the blossoming peach trees
or how she brightens this black tea I sip while reaching
for words to describe all I won't know.

Even the wind is slow to reveal a tip of truth
hidden beneath time's sand. What can I say
for those plum-colored poppies

lining the side of my house in late spring—
do they raise their heads
at my midday blaze of letters?

Yet, the painter does add her stroke of red,
the soprano a higher note than the common sparrow,
the sculptor his chip for some emerging image.

Perhaps these aren't the final *it* we can't resist
seeking, just a small slit in darkness
like those Advent candles we light before the appearance

of Christmas. Perhaps this is why
children lay claim to Christ's heart, him bidding
them come with their wide-eyed inquiries.

Isn't each question the starting mark to another
second with the One who squeals with delight
at every dangerous curve, never wants

the ride to end?

EXPONENT

\'ek-,spō-nənt\

Could you take a moment
to explain mathematics?
How a single person
can add to your sum?
I'm at a loss

in this equation—a zero some-
body gaining you nothing
so far as I can figure it.
That might be the problem—me
working in so much darkness.

Your hand's light
on the abacus, sliding each bead
where it's needed most.
Maybe my inability to multiply
means I'm in the middle

of a different calculation
where symbols do more than expand
or contract, but stand-in for
a spot in space
only one soul ever tends.

Not that I can make land
fall or ascend on my command
nor move it across
a continuum of time,
but I can leave my X

in this square foot of dust,
lay down my life
in lines forever intersecting
at a singular point
of view—one fixed in me

                    and risen
by a factor of you.

WED
    \'wed\

Why this veil of blue and scarlet,
this brocade of twisted linen turning
even the embroidered cherubim pale,

if when the cloud descends
everything winds up woolen
and without distinction?

Why call the craftsmen, send
for women who create curtains
of finest goat's hair, if you cover

the coverings of red-dyed ram skins
with a thick blanket no one can look through
or in?

Why shape an ornate lamp of gold,
set it on a carved stand, if we can't see
its shining, can't make out land for the fog?

Who can understand holiness
like that heavy ephod Moses
slipped over his head—

the onyx stones, amethyst, emerald, ruby
representing a people
neither slave nor free

just set apart in statutes,
married to a white heaviness by day,
a burning in the heart of the night?

VISITATION
\ˌvi-zə-ˈtā-shən\

Zacharias left the temple speechless,
no holy words echoing in tall pillars
just a haze of incense, the mind dazed
by the blow of Gabriel's trumpet.

Now his wife does all the talking,
offers a *Hail, Mary* for her husband
when the ark arrives at their door—
the Word of God sealed inside.

Try as he might, Zacharias can't
hitch a ride on angel's wings
to name the thing he heard. That cry
belongs to his soon-to-come son.

But that's jumping the storyline,
for now the baby leaps all over himself
in his cocoon of joy—an emerging voice
in movement not yet exclaiming dove

or pointing to a father's love rolling off
the tongue like water. Declaring instead,
in a mother's prayer, hope for the empty-
handed, for those who can't grasp

the horn, can't play in key
to unlock their own salvation.
She alone boldly inhales, then releases
until every inward is shouting out

Blessed be ...

UNVEILED
   \,ən-ˈvāld\

Clouds covered
the face of the moon
so no one could trace the outline

of those who terrorized
the church graveyard
turning over

headstones, defacing
the who, when, wherefore
of so many souls.

Score one for the Evil One
who cares for carved letters
knows no better glory

than chiseling stories
that leave scars
not moving us up

that mountain
to observe the sun—
the haloed hope of an unfading heart.

Now comes the part
where everything's parted
not unlike a split sea

we can walk through
or a curtain torn
in two, or that cloth

set askew
from the empty grave
wrappings. We can't help

but wonder
what those Disciples knew
as the cloud departed

and their eyes sparkled
like brides do
when the lace is lifted.

TRANSFIGURED
\tran(t)s-'fi-gyərd\

What are you hiding?
Some bright phase

beyond saturation,
perhaps? You,

a haze
we can't follow.

Is it inevitable that we fall
all over ourselves

slick as that apple
we can't grasp?

Name it a false reign,
if you will,

one that leaves us
hotter than before it came.

No matter
is not the matter,

rather that your condensing
feels condescending

at times. It's plain
confusing, really, you

crystallizing on angels' wings
in such a blinding light.

Peter sought to shelter in place
as if he could

figure out your figure,
but there is no point

of fullness reached
by going further.

You said, *Seek*
and you shall find

but we don't
even have to beg

to differ
because our vapors vary

in density—you
hovering over, us

dropping
every word like water

through our fingers.
In other words,

save your breath—
unless—hold it!

What's your touch
on my shoulder

revealing?

SEE
\\'sē\\

swine rush down
the steep bank, split
hooves and snouts
speeding past,
upending grass and stones.

Hell hath no fury
like a herd possessed
with its destination. Nothing
can stop their progress—
this sowing of the abyss.

No wonder the locals quickly
dismissed Jesus. Wouldn't we too?
As if we could ship off fear, float away
every pending precipice.
But the tipping point

hogs our attention
like that mighty Leviathan
breaching the sea.
Maybe there's no such thing
as out of sight and mind

just a fine line between
cliff and water
that breath we catch
with a kite—its tail uncurling
in the wind.

RESURRECTION
\,re-zə-'rek-shən\

In spring, when the remnant of snow
shrinks back into the shadows
of your small porch

you hand me hand tools, clay pots,
a lone packet of seeds then heave
the heavy bag of dirt to hip

so you can grip the sliding
glass door handle.
Now outside, just past

the equinox, just past
the capacity of coats
to make clumsy our movements,

we begin. You pouring out
soil, me hollowing little
holes

with a spade. And, finally,
with the slow tip
of your wrist, they slide onto

my outstretched palm
brown and lifeless,
tiny specks

of nothingness I sow
in each space   each opening
hungry for fullness.

Later, when grandpa asks, you'll say
we planted wishes. I'll smile,
look away—out the window

beyond the buried bodies, beyond
the sun now hidden
beneath the horizon

to that moment of Lupine,
Coreopsis, Shasta Daisy,
to that last day dream vivid

in violet and orange
and the softest pink
of an unfallen petal.

QUERY
 \'kwir-ē\

Is this the first time I've been here before?
Standing at this crossroad with its arrowed sign pointing
every way at once? More or less, you might say,

at the center of a paradox—the heart beating love
at its own game, the same blood pumped
into two legs—one moving left, the other right.

A slight contradiction in terms of peace—
that wars ceasing to be fought in person
are no less personal—land bought

or stolen with a paper and pen-
knife carving a compass in someone else's tree.
They're tapping that life-blood now sap

spread liberally on the streets until I'm stuck
moving in place. Yes, I'm making haste
toward stasis, am living to die. Why shouldn't I

carry this cross in my flesh
like that blue-black tattoo I got on my hip
when turning eighteen? I didn't ask then

if the burning would last forever,
hidden from sight. How is light so heavy
you can't lift it in a single gaze?

Even when naked, you tracing the outline
with your finger, finding us samely-orientated,
but different, I couldn't help but wonder

if this is what Christ meant
when he said the lost are found,
that those who give up everything

will be filled-in.

PROCREATION

\ˌprō-krē'āsh(ə)n\

The absence of issue
is an issue for Abram.

As if the presence of a problem
is the progeny he names with a laugh.

But it's not
the mandrake root which animates

an affair into a first born son.
That's some lesser magic

making an end run around circumcision
and the covenant with One who discharges

flesh on His command.
This produces an heir of contention

between Sarai and Hagar resulting in
a predictable jettison that solves nothing

so far as we can see. Thankfully,
we don't have to look further than the dust

on the feet of the three men
who arrived at Abram's tent

proclaiming a proof not in the sum
of old ages but in a someone beyond

man-made solutions, beyond
figuring out the stars, charting

their courses as we do with children
arranging them one after the next

in a doorframe to measure their height
with a pencil-thin line.

But outcomes aren't best measured
in the rings of a tree, in branches that reach

for eternity. Life works backwards
to the source—a force in favor of abundance,

of a multitude vast   and growing.

OMINOUS
\'ä-mə-nəs\

In the absence

of Moses, Aaron missed the signs
in the wilderness
got lost in the shine
of an earlobe.

Evil's not bound
to the dark, can be heard on loop
in daytime murmurs, glows gold
in collected ear-rings.

Beelzebub didn't utter a word
as Aaron worked his graving tools
to craft the molten calf
that caught the camp aflame.

In a crazed dance
the people arose as one
to worship a blazing
nothing,

the thick smoke ascending
to fill God's nostrils
until he smote them,
smashing each mis-

guided soul into embers
that still tingle our spines
every time we feel
the strong presence

of an absence.

NUMINOUS
\'nü-mə-nəs\

I want to feel
the storm inside—

summer song
of grey-green sky

rush
of inner electricity

throng
of wild rain

Come
Holy Awe—

O voice
of hallowed air

fingers
of keen light

body
of stirred water

I want to be warmed
and left shivering

MEDIUM
\\'mē-dē-əm\\

In the middle of the night
he came to En-dor—to the eye
that looks back as if all was before.

But he couldn't find her
in the blackness that spread
from the hills of Jezreel

to his mind. He called out her name
conjuring her from the house
like a rabbit from a hat.

She quickly read fear in his face—
that dark sphere seeking
the soothing word of a soothsayer

who can bend the laws of time,
mystify the clock, to bring up
the desired man.

This was no intermediate demand,
no tepid turning of the dial to channel
a temperate voice. A prophet

commands power from the source
and her small hands caught the sun,
for a moment possessed the core.

Years later, near her end,
she couldn't recall Saul's face
but still felt the spinning

in her abdomen at midnight—
the circling of a center
always in sight

but never within   reach.

LISTING
\\'li-stiŋ\\

In giving grievances against God
bullets serve best as holy missals,
a litany of pockmarks
on the upturned face of a page.

- darkness remains dark for those in the dark
  - free isn't free for the embodied
  - life's a lark for One with a legion of angels
    - a mystery never warms sheets on a cold night

Might I go on?

- gravity attracts indiscriminately
  - unfulfilled promises dig unfillable holes
- always means not occasionally
  - heat creates no sweetness in the burned

Shall I go on?

- holiness and shame are the same undressing before witnesses
  - inviting higher induces a lie
  - still means both motionless and not yet, rendering us useless
- faith begs trust while omniscience asks not a damned thing

Will I go on?

Or is this a sure fire way
to expire—
buckshot and bleeding
careening toward

- that

- wide

- pebbled

- path?

KINDLED
\\'kin-dᵊld\\

It's that time of year when the rising sun
aligns with my line of sight to blind me
during my morning commute.

I've entered the "visor-down dimension"
as my teenage daughter deems it
as if she already understood the blind trust

of motherhood—how my heart burns more
after I drop her at school, leave her
to turn the corner into her own vibrancy.

I mind the out-of-sight, grip the wheel tighter
as if I could wind the world in reverse
until the past is a future I might look forward to.

But the east holds my gaze, has me wondering
how one blazing orb can both render the road
invisible and warm me. I think of Christ

who bowed and prayed toward a temple
he couldn't see, not blinking in the face
of the fire before him. It's said that faith

is belief in things unseen, so I lift my visor,
loosen my fingers and merge into traffic,
which is surprisingly light for a Tuesday.

JUBILEE
\\'jü-bə-(ₗ)lē\\

So far as we know
there was no horn blowing
when Jesus unrolled the scroll
to read the prophet's words.

When he broke the seal of his lips
one might have heard a wind,
felt a light touch of snow
as when a field of dandelions lets   go.

And, like him
who stood in synagogue, we rise
to offer our anthem
for every free thing—

the comet in the night sky,
the zip of the hummingbird,
the boys choir singing higher
than the highest heaven.

Even angels join in
tapping their toes seven times seven
as if the liberty of fifty
is nipping at their heels.

And maybe it is
as the leper dips in,
the sightless man sees,
the desperate touch stops blood,

a tomb-side command starts it flowing.
So goes the unwinding
of slavery, the binding of "no",
the unheralded field left fallow

but in time offering life
to every widow, orphan, outcast,
even the lone sparrow opening
a seed at the wild edge.

INSTRUMENT

\ˈin(t)-strə-mənt\

Plotting the distance to Damascus
doesn't require drafting tools
or a sophisticated measuring device
just one hell-bent fool following

the rules at any cost. A price
he gladly pays until losing sight
of the destination—missing the end
by miles of misspent days

driving in the wrong direction.
So he moves in darkness guided not
by some remote mechanism but a hand
holding him on course to the city

where he sits in a fixed space
calculating the span
from himself   to holiness
always coming up short.

He longs for more fingers,
an abacus, or a slide rule
to prove his intervals true,
but he can't erase his calculations,

can't compute the question:
Saul, why do you persecute me?
Curious how the sun flashed at that moment
then disappeared

as if the apparatus he needs to heed
isn't beyond but now placed within
like blood orbiting through his body,
like a fresh song circulating

beneath skin   and rising
the way a violin scales high
then falls at the end of a concerto
so everything thereafter is seen

anew.

HOST
\\'hōst\\

It's said
the one who visited
Mary that night

was pure light—
no pinions
pulsating the air,

no down
lifting her up.
A glow

into which she stepped—
a crossed threshold.
Inside,

a gnawing,
a creature unborn
but borne

already hearing
the siren of sin
with its echoes and echoes sounding out

but not entering
that small ark
where there's feasting

without words,
without biting
and mashing one another.

Food as light
as a wafer.
The drink circulates—

a rush she welcomed
with the heartbeat,
with the brightness

of an eternal sun.

GYRATE

\\'jī-,rāt\\

The sun can interpret tongues
of praise, even the slight rolling
of the servant maids' hips are golden.
Everything orbits the chest—

this ark carried high
into the heart of Jerusalem,
beating inside the king who sings, spins
in the new heat of the day.

Now with the son of God circling,
the linen ephod knows how to move,
hugs the corners, is loose
in the straightaways.

The king keeps time
with his feet, leaps over
stone ages and dark centuries.
All the while

the mercy seat glistens
with the perspiration of cherubim
clapping their wings,
holding the forever One

who draws the line of David,
pulls it like a loose string, unravels
the world until it's a top
that can't stop its twirling.

FLINT
   \'flint\

   They stoned Paul. ~ Acts 14:19

Steel on stone sparks
      So too stone on flesh

Yes, the flash of pain
      Yes, the sear on the surface—

The stacking of so much
      The light shines through

Like an inverted altar
      With the meat underneath

The rocks on top hot
      From their heaving source

Such volcanic flair
      Easily misses the mark though

Forgets to account for the tare
      Of the container carrying heat

Rising up with forty feet of flames
      Into the night sky

Once started
      Nothing will stop it

From tearing everything open
      Freeing even those buried in darkness—

Headstones tipped, tossed
     Aside with minimal effort

Who knew a sideways glance
     Could become such an inferno

There are so many cities still to go

ENLIGHTENMENT
\in-'lī-tᵊn-mənt\

Night knows no distinction,
bodies in motion or at rest,
the right hand or left
holding tight or letting go.

In black, everything slows
to silence, to a time as smooth
as this bed frame's sanded beams
which bear us nowhere
and everywhere.

The clock on the nightstand dares me
to doubt its countdown
but I'm caught up
in another dimension laying claim
to an hour not yet come

that came before
the first phase played out,
even before the wine gave out
and the chief steward offered
his high praise.

This darkness may not be dark
but a different revolution
where a rising's more a settling
into all that's already occurred,
into a blind seeing

like the kiss I offer
under the covers,
like your hidden heart
I know.

DESERTS
     \ di-'zərts\

Steering your car
towards the Sahara
won't help you
get your just ones.

Hanging out with jackals
or cozying up to an ostrich
won't position you to perfect
the perfect petit four.

There's no need for 40 years
to learn the way, nor a
French pastry chef looking
over your shoulder.

Your Gobi may have scarcely
an egg white and your soul
could make it just fine.
After all, every soufflé falls

in the face of the Face
who stretches no plumb line
to measure your center
only races to behold you

like an attentive mother
who knows
the recipe by heart,
and the heart.

Who understands
blowing sand
can cover
          or reveal.

COUNTENANCE
\\'kaủn-tᵊn-ən(t)s\\

At dusk I start to see
endless combinations of letters,
even poetry, can't free me,

won't unlock the next level
like a golden key   revealed
by the right incantation.

My soul magnifies the Lord

Mary sang like she could hang
the entire universe on that line—
catching some ancient breeze.

If I could freeze that moment
for later dissection
I might find her the microscope—

the light and lens through
which the whole world
bends.

But now I'm naming a body
of work, not just a chapter
with angelic hymns and wise men.

A completely new form
of thing that continually rings
as if it had no beginning

or end.
It's hard to take this
sitting down, so I stand

to gain a different
point of view—one
I can almost see through.

When will this night
be torn asunder?
Come, Lightning,

Thunder,
the Face
of the full moon.

BLISS
  \'blis\

A cabin in the woods
you drawn close

to this hand-hewn hearth
blowing into darkness

knowing a breath
when released

turns light
like the flaming wheel

in Daniel's vision
caught

not in sight
but inside the chest

where the heart beats molten
flowing

This renders no less wondrous
your appearance

out of night
our slow kiss

back-lit
by a contained blaze

The possibility remains
you forever

might fan a burning
not bound by time

or place—
this strand of forest

this hand in mine
with its new metal

glowing

AWAKENING
\ə-'wāk-niŋ\

You next to me still
except for the slow rise of your chest

like that rise of hill behind the house
which the sun's just beginning to crest.

I trace the pillow impression on your face
follow to its end—the corner of your lips

casting their rose-colored light,
snagging my edge.

The spray of hair across your forehead
makes me pull back the sheets—

a metamorphosis into this
now marveling creature

inches from your skin,
from the exquisite sea of you

I want to breathe deeply of,
dive in.

And then,
I knew

I should have said more last night.

INWARD

SANCTUARY

\\'saŋ(k)-chə-,wer-ē\\

Our hands hunger for sand,
straw, the stuff of bricks
to satiate an empty
space, raise an earthen praise:

Higher!

Such elevated ways
shit sky as fodder
for the next day's
lunar landing.

But some places don't fit
our palms as easily as trowels
or hammers—as if everything
consumed goes up

Higher!

What of the widow with nothing
save a small jar and jug—
even a prophet can't get far
on such short supplies.

And, yet, we might be surprised
to discover a substantial
rise when standing on just
two mites

Higher!

like that other widow
who put it all in—
hovering above the temple
because Jesus called up her bet.

Long prayers
make short stairs compared
to her windfall—that full
drop we must swallow to follow

Higher!

ABIDE
  \ə-'bīd\

A dream
or vision?
You in me,

your beryl body
a mountain stream
I can see through.

You part
my lips
like a sea.

There in
between
past slavery

and future strife
I hear
your words without

sound, your say
beyond say
and I

go
go
go

until
my breath's
stolen

and I am
stayed
in you.

MOUNT
  \'maůnt\

Surprised that Sinai sings
with the voice of the moon,
you'd sooner lie to his face
than embrace some mere reflection

of lightness. His falsetto
fails to move you higher
than where those two stones
drop, break into a thousand

glowing slivers
piercing skin but never fully
illuminating, never raising
the pitch or pace of the heart.

Even starting at the start
in that void, in that black space
where unsung words rest,
you can't hear yourself think

can't scale the sound within.
Where then can one go free
of fire at night, of descending
clouds, of that echo

resounding distant falls?
Wind doesn't give a damn
if the Law always calls
for an accounting.

It blows where it will
until you're a seasoned soprano
astride its thermal, holding

                        every high note.

EQUIPOISE
  \'e-kwə-,póiz\

Is dawn the most favorable light to lift a blessing from the hand
        of the Almighty?

Jacob might agree in principle, though, he wrestled
        through the night

to find his footing in a limp. The question remains
        in limbo then

is life a breaking into day or darkness, or some irregular
        equilibrium of the two

like an off-kilter kilter carrying to the Promised Land?
        Scripture says he strove

with God and prevailed, but did he exactly nail the dismount—
        ten out of ten toes

touching ground? After all, he's a known heel-grabber
        stealing the birthright

right out from under Esau. But the Lord foresaw the move,
        countered with a hip check

that left him leaning into the asymmetrical symmetry of faith
        where pain and love share

a same frame, are optimally
balanced in one new name.

ACKNOWLEDGEMENTS

Jane Wheeler and Nellie deVries held every word in this collection, weighing each on a scale of worthiness. The ones found wanting they helped me release for better ones, while the singing words they cheered with abandon. What word can I offer for such a gift except *gratitude*.

John and Hannah Marie Roberts have been the keeper of my words for many years now, holding them close to their chests in an embrace I can only describe as love. One of the greatest gifts of my life is to call them *friends*.

Keith McAdams has suffered my droning on (and on) about these poems for many years over numerous strolls and dinners. Keith, I owe you a meal where my words are few and the book we open is *you*.

Gregory Alan Isakov, Sandra McCracken, Over the Rhine, Bruce Springsteen, and The Tallest Man on Earth generously shared their words in song as I wrote these poems. Thank you for inviting me into your company and whispering sweet everythings in my ear buds. If some of my words appear like yours, recall that imitation is the sincerest form of flattery. And I mean more than to flatter, but *praise*.

Finally, to the Word made flesh—every word was yours first and will be yours in the end. Come forever *inward*.

www.ingramcontent.com/pod-product-compliance
Lightning Source LLC
LaVergne TN
LVHW041045080426
835511LV00028B/673